the
unicorn
in you

Advance Praise

"I could feel myself starting to live Josh's words as I read them, just by reading them. It's that simple, and that complex. Josh unpacks five foundational words we've all said millions of times but, it turns out, never really knew. By articulating for us precisely what kindness, gratitude, integrity, humility, and acceptance are and how to practice each of them in our daily lives, Josh makes the often elusive life of peace and joy feel utterly possible."

—JORDAN ROTH, Tony Award-winning producer
and President of Jujamcyn Theaters

"Josh Kramer has created a delightfully insightful, pitch-perfect guide to living a meaningful, loving, and joyous life. More creative than formulaic, Josh has woven together timeless narratives with epic life lessons to illustrate the many ways we can cultivate a deeper sense of happiness and well-being. The idea that happiness is fueled by our own kindness, gratitude, and acceptance is best articulated by someone who has been exploring and practicing these concepts all his life. I have known and admired Josh Kramer for thirty years. Josh values and practices loving kindness and personal growth in a way that makes it seem effortless. But these practices require both effort and intention. With a generous spirit, Josh has provided a straightforward, tangible approach. The Unicorn In You is a book everyone should read."

—RACHEL SONTAG, author of House Rules

"Fasten your seatbelt and get ready to unleash your inner unicorn! This powerful guide by Josh Kramer provides invaluable insights into how we can all become our best selves. At once profoundly heartfelt and enjoyable, this special book will help you to elevate your life and impact from the moment you pick it up. Don't be surprised if you end up gifting it to everyone you know!"

—BERI MERIC, CEO and Founder of IVY

the unicorn in you

a path to peace and joy

JOSHUA KRAMER

SPECIAL AREAS

THE UNICORN IN YOU
A Path to Peace and Joy

ISBN   978-1-5445-2817-5 *Hardcover*
        978-1-5445-2816-8 *Paperback*
        978-1-5445-2818-2 *Ebook*

For Joy

Contents

Introduction

On a bright, sunny Saturday in November 2019, I spent the afternoon attending my nephew's soccer game. The South Florida weather was perfect, with a warm gentle breeze blowing, and I found it surprisingly relaxing to watch this group of nine-year-old kids running around with reckless abandon and little regard for personal space or athletic precision.

There were of course numerous parents cheering, some more determined and spirited than others. And off to one side of the field, a bunch of kids who weren't on a soccer team, mostly siblings of the players, were running around and having fun on their own. Among them was my nephew's sister, my four-year-old niece.

The game had already begun by the time I arrived, so after I spotted my nephew on the field, I went to say hello to his sister. I found her in that grassy area beside the field, unselfconsciously basking in what seemed to be utter peace and joy. As I walked in her direction, I soon caught her eye. She gave a little squeal of delight and came sprinting toward me.

Once close, she leaped into my arms and gave me a big hug. When I put her down, I noticed the bright, colorful sneakers she was wearing, which matched the big smile on her face.

"I like your shoes," I said. "They're very colorful."

She showed them off with great pride.

"Are those rainbows?" I asked.

She shook her head. "No, they're not rainbows. They're *unicorns.*"

To prove it, she held one of the shoes up to give me a better look. Upon closer inspection, I realized that, indeed, the colorful design I'd taken to be a rainbow was in fact a bright image of a unicorn. The fantastical creature was leaping through the air with a vibrant smile on its face. For some reason, at that moment, the sight of those colorful, happy unicorn shoes struck me. It may seem strange, but there was something about them, something light and free, something that I'd yearned for.

Now, to be fair, I wasn't pulling this association out of thin air. Like most people, I've always been aware of the mythology behind unicorns. They're usually portrayed as rare creatures with special powers, evoking awe and wonder and embodying qualities of enchantment, freedom, and wisdom.

Myth and legend have often depicted them as pure of heart and virtuous in deed, with the power to preserve light and beauty and restore life, but they are such uncommon creatures that their essence feels entirely out of reach. By extension, it's probably not too hard to understand why the unicorn seemed like such an apt metaphor for the peace and joy I'd long sought and struggled to find.

And all of this was triggered in my mind by a pair of size-ten children's Velcro shoes. Full disclosure: At that moment, I was briefly curious if they made an adult-size pair.

Months later, that connection between peace and joy and unicorns only became stronger in my mind. Fast forward to March 2020, right around the beginning of worldwide quarantines and social distancing. I was following the pandemic online, watching the news on TV, and hearing stories from other people. To say it felt surreal would be an understatement, and like most, I found I lacked the words to express my emotions.

I knew people were suffering, both personally and professionally, and many were losing their lives to the virus. Indeed, life now seemed especially fleeting. Wanting to give the situation the respect it deserved, I committed to looking deep within myself during this time so I could attempt to gain a better understanding of what mattered most.

Even before the crisis, I had always preached the importance of three things to myself and my loved ones: health, family, and time. When my grandmother was alive, she used to say, "If you have your health, you have your wealth." That sentiment stuck with me, and for many years, I felt blessed that I'd been fortunate enough to avoid any serious health problems. I'd always been a firm believer that any circumstance, no matter how bad, could always be worse, and no matter how bad I might have it, someone somewhere always had it worse. Thus, I've always appreciated the value of my health.

In addition to my health, my family was always extremely important to me. I'm fortunate to have a big, happy family, and I've always considered my friends and other loved ones extensions of that family. These cherished people in my life had always given me fuel for my existence because I knew I wasn't alone in the world and felt cared for by many. Not everyone could make that claim, and knowing that some lacked loving parents, siblings, or even friends, I was grateful for how vast my support system was.

In fact, because of my health and family, I always felt like I had all I needed. However, when the COVID crisis hit, I became even more acutely aware of a more precious commodity: time. Some days, time seemed to stand still. Other times, it flew by.

I never cared for the idea that we've slipped into something like the movie *Groundhog Day*, with the same thing happening over and over again. That view seemed too cynical. I much preferred Maya Angelou's perspective: "Today is a beautiful day. I have never seen this one before."

Indeed, I've always tried to greet each new morning as something special. And as time now took on a whole new meaning, suddenly we were all being faced with our own mortality. So I began to ask the question, "What am I going to do with whatever time I've got left? How can I make the most of it? How can I ensure I don't take it for granted?" These questions inspired me to start looking for the gifts that *this* time had to offer, and that, in turn, began a personal journey to find the peace and joy that my niece wore so proudly.

A Winding Road to Peace and Joy

The image I kept coming back to during this time was the unicorn, with its mythical purity, lightness, and ease of mind. It seemed as good a symbol as any for the peace and joy I longed to find, but how could I ever achieve them?

How could I even begin to take steps toward finding real, sustainable peace and joy in my life? I've always believed in the importance of the *journey*, but my personal journey over the years has been a long, frustrating trek through the "wellness wilderness."

For years, I had struggled to find a true and consistent sense of happiness; I could never seem to get out of my own head. I often found it difficult to shrug off the anxieties and burdens that weighed me down. Those struggles began at a relatively young age, though I lacked the awareness to understand what was affecting me, as well as the emotional resources to address them.

Moments of sadness were frequent, and when I sought advice from loved ones, I was usually encouraged to "cheer up," as if simply shrugging off these debilitating bouts was an option. Ignoring my anxieties didn't help, while digging in to understand them more closely often made things worse.

At the time, I found comfort in bookstores, getting lost in the sea of covers, pages, and topics, often in warm, quiet settings. That's how I came across my first self-help book—the first of many as it turned out. I read it and found it interesting, as I tried to grasp for some sense of hope. Soon I read another. And another. I was seeking answers, but I was too naive at the time to even know what the *questions* were.

What appealed to me about the potential of these books was the idea that I could take immediate control of my mental and emotional well-being. They offered me what felt like a lifeline in a raging sea, but ultimately all of my self-help study and practices yielded inconsistent and mostly unsteady results.

Many of the processes I learned were difficult to maintain because I was never entirely able to get out of my own head. For nearly twenty-five years, I struggled to simplify the role I played in my own well-being, which created a pattern of continuously seeking help elsewhere. In hindsight, I realize I was ill-equipped to dig in and look deeper at what lay at the root of my sadness and anxiety. Ultimately, it took a long time to come to terms with the reality that, like many others, I suffered from depression.

Although the self-help mechanisms I learned along the way

gave me some sense of temporary relief during the most difficult struggles, the darkness was overpowering, leaving me feeling utterly helpless. Overwhelmed and emotionally exhausted, I experienced a severe mental anguish that ultimately led to some physical ailments. Basic tasks, movements, and even thoughts were paralyzing, and if I'd had the strength, I would have begged for the pain to stop.

If you've had to endure this to any degree, you know how relentless and unbearable the feeling is. It's debilitating and frightening all at once, and even during the "better" times, the weight and presence of it hung over my head, as if I were holding my breath and waiting for its arrival. When you're in it, there seems to be no way out.

Gradually, I became more open and honest with myself about it and eventually more vulnerable and willing to discuss it. As a private person, it still wasn't easy, though even today the catharsis of writing about it continues to help ease the shame and embarrassment I once felt.

So how did things change? How was I able to turn the corner and start making progress on dealing with my sadness? I really can't say there was a single moment when it happened. The progress was so incremental that it's difficult to pinpoint a specific breakthrough, but after finding my way to a glimmer of light and catching what felt like the faintest breath of air, I slowly worked my way out of my own head. It was then that I began trying to clarify exactly what it was that I'd been searching for.

Although insufficient, at that time I would have settled for "I want to not feel bad." However, if you'd asked me what I *really* wanted, I probably would have said, "Happiness," despite it being so abstract and ill-defined in my mind that it felt unattainable. I'm not sure I appreciated that there were different types of happiness for me to pinpoint.

I began to look deeper within in an effort to determine what the happiness I sought in fact looked like. It took some time, but I eventually came to realize that what I truly desired wasn't really happiness but *peace and joy*. While I'd spent years looking for some process, some mechanism that would make me truly content, I finally grasped that the path to peace and joy was actually more of a *journey* than a process. Even though it took a while, that journey would soon lead me to a youth soccer game and a major discovery about what my destination looked like.

Now that the goals had been identified, I needed to define them more clearly. So what *are* peace and joy?

Peace: a stress-free state of security and calmness that comes when there's no fighting or war, everything coexisting in perfect harmony and freedom.[1]

Joy: the emotion evoked by well-being, success, or good fortune, or by the prospect of possessing what one desires.[2]

Those definitions work well, but on a more personal level, the elements of peace that resonated most deeply with me were "harmony and balance," while joy seemed to arise from the peace that was cultivated within. I think peace and joy, understood this way, are things that almost all of us are seeking, whether we realize it or not, and most of us have an unclear approach as to how to obtain them.

---

[1] https://www.vocabulary.com/dictionary/peace

[2] https://www.merriam-webster.com/dictionary/joy

Reflecting on the processes of the self-help programs I'd studied, I found many were simply not very instinctive. To me, the real question became, how can we learn to live in an organic way, more freely and naturally, without obsessing over the results or benefits and without overanalyzing everything?

The answer: By acting in a way that is foundational to who we are. In other words, *being* rather than *doing*.

This breakthrough then prompted another significant mindset shift.

To be light, you first have to be solid.

That's what a foundation does for you—it makes your whole life stable and solid. If we lay the right foundation for our lives, a foundation for *being* rather than *doing*, then we will be able to act naturally and live our lives in a way that is free-flowing and light, without having to overthink what we do and without having artificial processes controlling our daily routines. And so long as it's the *right* foundation, this lighter, freer way of living will give us a lasting peace and joy that is more durable and sustaining.

Once I understood what I really wanted, it seemed ambitious but within reach. I now had to be clear about which principles best contributed to the right foundation. And what did I determine?

That to get to the core of what I really needed, I had to get out of my own self-absorbed head and begin focusing on being *kind* to others, being *grateful* for what I have, acting with *integrity*, living *humbly*, and *accepting* life as it is rather than regretting how it isn't.

As simple as it sounds, I believe that's the most direct path to peace and joy: *kindness, gratitude, integrity, humility, and acceptance.* And it's this path that I will share with you in the following chapters.

To be sure, this approach is not intended to be a professional "positive psychology" methodology, nor is it the result of clinical studies. Rather, it is a practical perspective that is both sensible and uncomplicated, with universal appeal and timeless insights that can move you closer to peace and joy in your life, no matter what you're going through. Intentionally, the tone is meant to be that of a gentle reminder and thoughtful guide.

For each of the five principles, we will distill one key ingredient that drives them. For kindness, we need *compassion*. For gratitude, we must have *awareness*. To have integrity, the focus should be on *decency*. With humility, *perspective* is needed. And acceptance requires *flexibility*.

The content shared in these pages is geared for laypeople and written in accessible language. The five key principles don't require much hard work or deep thinking. They're principles that anyone can embrace in difficult times. Your work is to make them the foundation of your being, building the everyday structures of your life on top of kindness, gratitude, integrity, humility, and acceptance. We'll discuss some practical ways of doing this, but in the end, they have to become foundational to *your* life in a way that works best for you.

Louise Hay once wrote, "I don't fix my problems. I fix my thinking and then my problems fix themselves." With that sentiment in mind, the principles I've set forth are intended to offer an adjustment to your thinking. They will challenge the standards you feel are most important and offer a path to peace and joy through virtues and values that can stand the test of the time. It's a back-to-basics approach that simplifies in order to strengthen.

Building a Foundation

For many of us, it's often easier to simply react to circumstances in life without a foundation on which to create consistent behavior. At the same time, we are so inwardly focused and directed at *self* that we feel constantly overwhelmed by cares, worries, and anxieties.

To address this problem, the foundation I will present has as its most essential ingredient *selflessness*, which becomes the unifying thread between each of the principles, emphasizing the need to let go of the burden of ego, get out of your own head, and remove self-absorption.

The five principles cut through the considerable layers of information that often cloud our life experience and concentrate more precisely on (1) how you treat others, (2) how you appreciate what you have, (3) how you maintain your core values, (4) how you view yourself, and (5) how you accept things in the world.

By learning and applying these principles, you will be able to act instinctively, rather than having to rely on any kind of mechanism or external practice that can itself become tiresome. The principles are foundational and therefore *fundamental* to our being. Let's look at each of them briefly.

First, we have **kindness**. In many ways, kindness is the key to all of the other principles—and everything else in life. As the fourteenth Dalai Lama has famously said, "Be kind whenever possible. It is always possible." It can't get much clearer than that.

Second, we have **gratitude**. This feeling builds directly off kindness, creating a natural flow for being. Ultimately, gratitude depends on developing an awareness of what you have in life and the good that is already around you.

Third, we have **integrity**. This foundational principle provides a solid basis for consistent decision making. It's driven by decency, which means recognizing and living your core values and forgoing the rationalization that ignores basic honor and respect.

Fourth, we have an underappreciated principle: **humility.** This principle has much to do with your perspective on life, so we will explore how it can recenter your purpose by reducing the size and scope of misplaced self-importance. Humility creates a context for everything you experience by helping you understand your own significance—and insignificance—in the grand scheme of things.

Finally, we have **acceptance**, a principle that is about our ability to cope with change. By embracing flexibility, we allow ourselves to accept *what is* and let go of *what isn't*. This is critical for feeling light and free because it roots us in reality and relieves us of impractical expectations.

And so it is possible, with open-mindedness, to make a conscious decision to build a foundation for peace and joy in a way that is both manageable and effective. As for that unicorn, it serves as a valuable and inspiring symbol on this journey because it embodies the combination of these principles, which are as rare as the unicorn itself. So let's take the first step to discovering the unicorn in you.

What Matters Most?

The idea for this five-principle foundation first entered my mind when I was asked a thought-provoking question. It happened at a business luncheon I attended in which prominent author Ryan Holiday was scheduled to speak about his then-newly released book *Stillness Is the Key.*

As good fortune would have it, I was placed at the same table as the guest of honor. During our meal, a discussion topic was posed to everyone which effectively asked, "In your life, what matters most to you, and what do you know for sure?"

I had an immediate and instinctive answer, but true to my personality, I was reluctant to speak up first. However, Ryan eventually looked at me and asked if I had anything to share. I hesitated a moment, then said, "I think kindness is pretty much everything for me." I elaborated a little further on how kindness was the principle that guided me in life, especially in terms of how I treated other people— as well as how I treated myself, though this was often the greater struggle.

After the discussion ended, Ryan rose to give his presentation. He shared some compelling ideas on stillness, answered some questions, and then the event wrapped up. I stayed behind afterward so I could tell him how much I'd enjoyed the afternoon. We chatted a bit, and then he headed down the stairs to the exit, while I collected my coat.

Less than a minute later, I heard someone coming back up the steps. It was Ryan, and he was holding something in his hand.

"Here, this is for you," he said, handing me a bronze coin about the size of a silver dollar. "You mentioned that kindness is your thing, so I thought you might like this."

I looked at the coin. On one side, it had the inscription, "Summum Bonum," a Latin expression meaning "the highest good." On the other side, it read, "Just that you do the right thing, the rest doesn't matter."

It was a simple expression, but I was struck by how meaningful this small gesture felt to me. Someone doing something nice for me without expecting anything in return lightened my whole day—and likely made him feel good as well. That's the simple power of kindness.

It was a moment I would come to think about often as I formulated the ideas presented in this book, though at the time, I still had a long way to go. Coincidentally, or perhaps not, exactly thirty days after that encounter, I found myself at a youth soccer game watching my four-year-old niece playing in the grass in her unicorn sneakers.

So let's get into that feeling—that peaceful, joyful, sparkling unicorn place. Yes, we can get there. I believe we can *live* there.

It all starts with kindness.

> *"People will forget what you said,*
> *people will forget what you did, but*
> *people will never forget how*
> *you made them feel."*
>
> —MAYA ANGELOU

Chapter One

Kindness

"Kindness is the language which the deaf
can hear and the blind can see."

—Mark Twain

O nce upon a time, the wind and the sun had an argument about which of them was the more powerful of the two. Looking below, they saw a traveler walking along the road, wrapped in a long cloak.

"Let's make a wager," the sun said. "Whichever one of us can make the traveler remove his cloak shall be declared the winner and, therefore, the stronger of the two."

"So be it," the wind replied, agreeing to the wager. "I'll go first!"

And with that, the wind sent a cold, howling blast down upon the traveler, whipping his cloak and his hair and chilling him. The traveler shivered and wrapped the cloak even tighter around him. The wind blew harder and colder, almost bowling the man over, but the traveler merely clutched the cloak shut with his hands and trudged on.

No matter how long the wind blew, no matter how cold or fierce the blast, the traveler would not remove the cloak. He only held it shut more tightly and kept going. All of the wind's efforts proved futile.

"I give up," the wind said finally. "No matter how fiercely I blow, he simply will not remove his cloak."

"Very well," the sun replied. "It's my turn."

So the sun began to shine. At first, the sun's beams were gentle, and the traveler found the sudden warmth pleasant, especially after the bitter cold. Eventually, he let go of the cloak and let it hang a little more loosely on his shoulders.

The sun's rays then grew warmer, and the traveler began to mop his brow. Finally, he took the cloak off and sat down in the shade of a tree beside the road to rest.

"I did it," said the sun. "It was my warmth that caused him to remove his cloak. I win."

This fable by Aesop was well-known in ancient Greece, but its simple point holds just as true today as it did then, that kindness and gentle persuasion can win where force and bluster often fail. It's the power of kindness to transform lives, change hearts, and heal wounds that has been recognized by wise people throughout the centuries.

As philosopher and physician Albert Schweitzer once said, "Constant kindness can accomplish much. As the sun makes ice melt, kindness causes misunderstanding, mistrust, and hostility to evaporate."

Kindness and Compassion

Kindness is the first and most important of all the core principles we will discuss in this book. Roald Dahl, author of *Charlie and the Chocolate Factory*, once wrote, "I think probably kindness is my number one attribute in a human being. I'll put it before any of the things like courage, or bravery, or generosity, or anything else. Kindness—that simple word. To be kind—it covers everything, to my mind. If you're kind, that's it."

A more contemporary angle, from a story that circulated on social media in 2020, illustrates why kindness comes first.

A professor gave a balloon to each of her students. She had each student inflate their balloon, write their name on it, and throw it out into the hallway. Once all of the balloons were scattered in the hall, she gave the students two minutes to find their own balloons. They rushed out into the hall and began to look, but despite a hectic search, the whole class couldn't find their respective balloons in the time limit.

Finally, the professor said, "Okay, let's try again, but this time, instead of looking for your own balloon, just grab whatever balloon you find, see whose name is written on it, and give it to that person."

Once again, the students threw their balloons out into the hallway. Then they rushed out to collect them. This time, instead of each student looking for their own balloon, they grabbed the first one they came across, read the name written on it, and gave it to the correct person. In this way, everyone received their own balloon long before the time limit was up.

At the end, the professor told the students, "These balloons are like happiness. We will never find it if everyone is looking for their own. But if we care about other people's happiness, we'll find ours, too."

That's the power of kindness, and I believe that at the core of kindness is compassion. The formal definition of compassion is, "sympathetic consciousness of others' distress together with a desire to alleviate it."[3] In other words, compassion is a *recognition*, while kindness is the *action* that follows. The former provides the fuel that drives the latter.

In the context of our story, imagine a scenario where the students helped each other gather up the balloons without being instructed to do so by the professor. In that scenario, it would be simple acts of kindness driven by mutual empathy for one another.

You've probably heard the term "random acts of kindness." It originated as a saying coined by a journalist named Anne Herbert back in 1982, which was in turn a play on the journalistic phrase "random acts of violence." The original full saying was, "Practice random kindness and senseless acts of beauty."

In truth, kindness is almost never random. Even though the recipients of our kind deeds might be unknown to us,

---

[3] https://www.merriam-webster.com/dictionary/compassion

possibly strangers during a chance encounter, acts of kindness are almost always intentional. Of course, although kindness is ideally something we actively choose, each act of kindness doesn't need to be a conscious decision—they can be done instinctively and naturally.

To be clear, kindness is not just about *acts*; it's about our essence and being. However, in order to make it a core principle in our lives, it's important to reframe it in our minds so we see it as intentional, purposeful, and driven by compassion. We empathize with people when we are willing to put ourselves in their shoes and try to understand how they're feeling, which promotes and perpetuates kind behavior toward them.

Without compassion, kindness is hollow, and our attempts at it may be misguided. If we want to help someone, we must be able to see things from their perspective so we can understand what they will view as kindness in the moment. It's with genuine and heartfelt benevolence that this becomes possible.

Compassion is something we all have access to. It's not merely the result of some inherited genetic trait or a personality quirk that only a select few possess. On the contrary, we are all capable of compassion, and it comes from a conscious willingness to see other human beings and try to understand how they're feeling. It's projecting our own conscious selves into their lives and experiences and then acting toward them accordingly.

The Path of Kindness

So how does compassion-driven kindness lead to peace and joy?

1. Kindness Has Health Benefits

If there were ever a valid, personal reason to embrace kindness, it's the health benefits that result from it. As mentioned in the Introduction, this book and the perspective shared in it are not the result of clinical studies, and my purpose isn't to provide medical findings. However, there have been numerous studies by qualified medical professionals that reveal a link between kindness and decreased blood pressure and reduced stress levels. Also, according to the Mayo Clinic, "Kindness can increase your sense of connectivity with others, which can directly impact loneliness, improve low mood and enhance relationships in general."[4]

For many of us, our baseline of positive mental health fluctuates to a degree that can be unsettling at best and deeply painful at worst, but kindness provides a number of advantages to aid in our welfare that costs very little. Enhanced relationships alone can have an enormous impact on our psyche, reducing feelings of isolation and providing a foundation for improved well-being. Indeed, when you consider the physical and mental health benefits, it becomes clear that kindness may be the kindest thing you can do for yourself.

2. Kindness Provides Pleasure

Ironically, showing kindness to others can be self-serving because it gives us what we might call a helper's high. You probably know this from experience. It simply makes us feel good to do something nice for someone else. As the old

---

[4] https://www.mayoclinichealthsystem.org/hometown-health/
speaking-of-health/the-art-of-kindness

proverb says, "Kindness is its own reward." Yes, it impacts the other person, possibly in a profound way, and sometimes, one small act of kindness at the right moment can change a person's life. But we can do it for our own pleasure as well.

Supporting this idea, kindness has been shown to release dopamine, the chemical messengers of the brain that give us a feeling of euphoria and well-being. That leads to improved mood and has even been called "the body's natural pain killer."[5]

As the article from the Mayo Clinic points out, "Kindness has been shown to increase self-esteem, empathy and compassion, and improve mood."[6] We not only feel better, but we feel better about *ourselves*. This is incredibly important, because so many people who struggle to find peace and joy are struggling with self-esteem. They simply don't feel good about themselves, and this despair seeps into many other areas of their lives. Kindness becomes a plausible remedy for this sorrow.

---

[5] Ibid.

[6] Ibid.

3. *Kindness Lightens Your Mind*

As most of us know all too well, one reason we lack peace and joy is because we reside too much in our own minds. By focusing on kindness toward others, you get out of your own head and focus on others rather than solely on yourself. This helps you to feel lighter because you're not constantly thinking about your own burdens, troubles, needs, or wants. Indeed, as the Mayo Clinic article recommends, "Looking for ways to show kindness can give you a focus activity, especially if you tend to be anxious or stressed in some social situations."[7]

This can be useful as a form of distraction, taking us from the worries that consume us to an altruism that gives us something else to ponder. Oftentimes, this interruption, however brief, gives us a reprieve and temporary relief from the weight of our ongoing thoughts. The struggles that consume us are put on hold, if only for a moment, and the resulting positive consequences of our kindness can help to alter our point of view when we return to our own concerns.

---

[7] https://www.mayoclinichealthsystem.org/hometown-health/
speaking-of-health/the-art-of-kindness

Of course, the high you feel from a single act of kindness doesn't last forever. It's something that needs to be repeated. When you make the "repetition of kindness" a central part of your lifestyle, you wind up spending much more time living in that happier and healthier place. It's a bit like developing a muscle through repetitive exercise, which also requires dedication and commitment.

In the end, even though kindness is ideally shown with the best of intentions, we may find it easier to manifest it on a more consistent basis if we're mindful of its benefits for ourselves.

The Way to Compassion

There are a few effective ways that we can practice compassion-driven kindness.

1. Release Your Own Judgments

In this context, when we talk about judgment, we're talking about estimating the worth of others, particularly in regard to condemnation—and comparison with ourselves.

In the same way that compassion fuels kindness, judgment fuels negative emotions such as envy, anger, sadness, and the types of comparisons that don't really serve any useful purpose. Perhaps you've heard the old expression, "Comparison is the thief of joy."

When we sit in judgment of others, we hold on to negative emotions that are decidedly unhelpful. Condemning others and feeling angry, sad, or bitter toward them doesn't add anything constructive or positive to your life. So if you're aiming for joy, you might as well let these judgments go.

The next time you look at someone, let go of the need to make any assumptions about their worth, value, or qualities. Resist the urge to respond with pessimism or negativity about them. How do you do this? As the saying goes, "Before you judge a person, walk a mile in their shoes." Instead of making assumptions, try to understand what it would be like if you were in their place—if you'd had their experiences, feelings, struggles, and circumstances.

We all have the natural capacity to do this because we all have a sense of imagination. As a mental exercise, simply imagine changing places with other people. Think through their circumstances and try to imagine what it would feel like to experience them. Instead of taking another person's behavior at face value, be curious about what might be going on in their life and how those factors might contribute to that behavior.

The catch is that we can never truly know what happens behind anyone's closed doors. We never know what other people have gone through, or how they have gotten to the point in life where they're at now. But we can learn to give people the benefit of the doubt by imagining what it would be like to switch places with them.

It might be easier to feel pessimistic toward others, but assuming the worst contributes nothing useful or productive to our lives. It certainly won't get you closer to real, lasting peace and joy. As the famous Greek philosopher Plato avowedly said, "Be kind, for everyone you meet is fighting a hard battle."

2. Practice "Prosocial" Behavior

The term "prosocial" was created by social scientists in order to draw a contrast with antisocial behavior. Prosocial behaviors are those actions intended to help other people. They embody a concern for other people's feelings, with a specific focus on their well-being. Having a mindset of compassion will make it easier to connect with feelings that identify opportunities to actively help others.

First, take note of what's happening in any particular situation, then use compassion to understand how you might help other people in that situation. Put more simply, when compassion kicks in, you'll start to look for ways to help and then make a conscious decision to offer that help.

Prosocial behavior creates a sense of perpetual motion. It is fed by compassion, which then reinforces and deepens empathy. The key is to pay attention in social situations and identify those opportunities to act in ways that will be well received and contribute to the well-being of others.

An additional piece to this puzzle is the concept of the *greater good*. This has much to do with the idea of benefiting more people than yourself, and when we talk about prosocial behavior, it is ultimately inspired by this philosophy. It's a concept that will have practical uses when discussing the principle of integrity, though there are clear applications as it relates to kindness. In both, we begin to see the thread of *selflessness* tying these principles together through the vital connection between sacrifice and the greater good.

3. Allow for Emotional Vulnerability

When we allow ourselves to be emotionally vulnerable, we become open to the possibility of being emotionally wounded. Perhaps that is why so many people resist it, building up mental and emotional walls to keep others at bay.

If you really want to get closer to peace and joy, you're going to have to break down some of those walls. Specifically, to become a more compassionate person, you have to lay down your fears and insecurities and allow people in.

Allowing yourself to be vulnerable is scary—after all, nobody wants to be hurt—but letting other people in creates a necessary connection for developing a greater sense of compassion for them. So how do you make yourself more vulnerable? The first step is to be completely honest with yourself about how *you* feel. Then transfer your deep feelings into your perception of other people. Remember, we're all human beings, so it stands to reason that our feelings are actually quite similar.

If you get in touch with your own feelings, you will learn to identify them better in others and, as a result, can empathize with what others are going through. The idea of being vulnerable and going "deep" is much in vogue these days, but its benefits are not just for their own sake. We learn more about ourselves when we become more open, which allows for more profound and meaningful growth.

That growth is what creates the space within us to develop the compassion that is necessary for kindness. It's a process that continues as we broaden the scope of our understanding of others and evolve into better versions of ourselves.

A Kind Act Is Never Wasted

Since we opened the discussion on kindness with one of Aesop's fables, it seems appropriate to recount our own version of another famous fable as we close. It's that well-known tale about kindness called *The Mouse and the Lion.*

A great lion lay sleeping in the forest, his head resting on his paws. A tiny mouse was passing through the forest and accidentally walked close to the lion. Noticing the enormous predator, the mouse was startled and tried to run away, but in his haste, he ran across the lion's nose.

Roused from sleep, the lion grabbed the mouse in his paw, intending to kill him.

"Spare me, sir," the little mouse begged.

"Why should I spare you?" the lion said. "You woke me up when I was sleeping comfortably. Furthermore, I am a predator, and you are prey."

"Please, sir," the mouse said. "If you let me go, I promise that I will repay you someday!"

The lion was amused by this and laughed. "How could a tiny mouse ever repay me?" he said. "There is nothing you can do for me because there is nothing I need from you. Besides, you are small and weak."

Nevertheless, he looked upon the helpless creature and took pity on him. Opening his paw, he let the mouse go free. The little mouse quickly ran off into the forest, and the lion laid his head down again to sleep.

A few days later, the lion was stalking prey when he got caught in a hunter's net. The ropes pulled taut, and he was hoisted off the ground. Even though he struggled and thrashed, he was unable to free himself. Instead, the more he struggled, the more tightly the ropes wrapped around him. Fearing that the hunter would come along and kill him, the frustrated lion began to roar with helpless anger.

Meanwhile, the little mouse was in another part of the forest, but he heard the lion's roar, and he could tell that the great predator was distressed.

"Perhaps now I can repay the lion for his mercy toward me," the mouse thought.

He set off through the forest toward the source of the sound. When he got there, he found the lion struggling helplessly in the net.

"You spared my life once upon a time," the mouse said. "Now I am going to save yours."

And with that, he climbed up onto the net and began gnawing at the ropes with his tiny, sharp teeth. Soon, the ropes came apart, and the lion was able to pull himself out of the net.

"You laughed when I said I would repay you," the mouse said, "but now you see that even a mouse can help a lion."

The mouse and the lion parted ways in friendship, each having helped the other.

The moral of the story: A kind act is never wasted.

Perhaps we can approach the story from a slightly different perspective. Why should a lion, an apex predator, allow a tiny mouse to go free? Because in that moment, he felt a glimmer of empathy for the mouse and decided to *act* on that feeling.

Now, in the story, the lion's compassion-driven kindness led to a reciprocal act of kindness that literally saved his life. However, kindness doesn't always repay us in that way. Most of the time, it repays us by that endorphin rush, that sense of self-satisfaction and pleasure that comes from alleviating the suffering of others. You see, even if the recipient of your kind deed doesn't or can't repay you, kindness lightens your burdens and becomes its own reward.

As Anne Frank wrote in her famous diary, "No one has ever become poor by giving." This is certainly true of kind deeds. There are considerable mental, emotional, and physical benefits of showing kindness to others that make it worthwhile, even if the little mouse never returns to free you from the hunter's net.

The reduced stress and improved self-esteem alone can be profoundly life-changing once you begin to practice kindness. When you let go of judgment, embrace a prosocial mindset about other people, putting yourself in their shoes and becoming more vulnerable, you end up giving to yourself just as much as you give to others. This is why kindness is the central and beginning principle for building a foundation of peace and joy. In a sense, you don't need to be paid back because you have already rewarded yourself.

Remember the wager between the sun and the wind? The wind thought it could get the traveler to remove his cloak by blasting him as fiercely as possible. It didn't try to understand the feelings and experiences of the traveler. Like those who lack kindness, he tried to induce behavior change through harshness and force.

In contrast, the sun looked down upon the traveler and thought, "I don't have to be harsh. He's shivering against the cold and probably tired from walking. If I give him some warmth, he will remove the cloak and take a rest."

Even though it wasn't fully an act of kindness within the context of the story, we can see a metaphor for gentleness in the warmth of the sun's beams. He understood what the traveler needed, provided it softly, and the traveler acted accordingly. There's a power in kindness, and even more so when it's driven by compassion. People want to bask in the glow of genuine empathy.

To this point, Abraham Lincoln once wrote, "Kindness is the only service that will stand the storm of life and not wash out. It will wear well and be remembered long after the prism of politeness or the complexion of courtesy has faded away."

Just as the mythical unicorn is often attributed with healing powers, kindness often brings healing both to the giver and the receiver. Simple acts of kindness can change lives. Or as English author Sarah Fielding put it, "Words of kindness are more healing to a drooping heart than balm or honey."

Once we're committed to kindness through compassion, there's a direct connection between kindness and the next principle: *gratitude*, which is driven by *awareness*. When we're grateful and aware of what we have, we will find it easier to be kind.

*"Do things for people not because
of who they are or what they do in return,
but because of who you are."*

—Harold Kushner

Chapter Two

Gratitude

*"Gratitude is a divine emotion:
it fills the heart, but not to bursting;
it warms it, but not to fever."*

—CHARLOTTE BRONTË

A ccording to the ancient Greek writer Ovid, Midas was a king of Phrygia, an ancient city in west-central Anatolia (located in modern-day Turkey), who was famous for his great wealth. One day, he showed hospitality to a satyr named Silenus, and as a result, the god Dionysus offered him a reward of whatever he wished for. And Midas, being greedy despite his great wealth, asked for the ability to turn anything he touched into solid gold.

Dionysus warned him that such a power would be perilous, but Midas insisted on it. Finally, his wish was granted, and Midas tested his power, touching a small twig. Before his eyes, the twig transformed from wood into shiny gold. The king was amazed, and he soon went about touching all sorts of things, as his lust for gold immediately filled him.

For a while, Midas had the time of his life using his power, the "Midas touch," to create more gold than he knew what to do with. But eventually, he grew hungry. He ordered his servants to bring him some food, but when he grabbed the food with his hands, it turned to gold. He then tried picking the food up with a fork and putting it into his mouth, but it turned to gold on his tongue.

He then became thirsty, so he had his servants bring him a cup of wine. When he picked it up, the cup and the wine it contained became solid gold.

"What am I going to do?" he wondered. "If I can't eat and drink, I will die!"

Suddenly, his wish didn't seem like such a good idea. Midas slumped in his chair, lamenting his condition and the rumble of his empty belly.

At that moment, his young daughter entered the room, and seeing that her father was sad, she rushed to his side. He tried to warn her, but it was too late. She threw her arms around him to comfort him, and instantly, she turned into solid gold.

Horrified, Midas rose from his seat and fled his palace. He ran to the river, weeping bitterly, but the sand on the riverbank turned as yellow as fool's gold beneath his feet. Falling to his knees, he prayed to Dionysus and begged to be delivered from the curse of his own greed.

"If only I'd appreciated what I already had," he said, "instead of lusting after what I did not have. I no longer want this power! It has robbed me of all joy and taken the things that mattered most in my life."

Dionysus heard his prayer and granted his request, making it so that his very tears washed away the curse as they fell into the river. As he rose, Midas noticed that the ground had turned back to normal sand beneath him. He returned home to find that everything else he had touched had turned back to normal as well.

When he entered the dining hall, his daughter was waiting for him. King Midas hugged her tightly, and this time he wept tears of relief. His lust for gold was gone, and he felt grateful for all of the things he had in his life.

This story brings us to the second foundational principle that leads to peace and joy: *gratitude*. It is a feeling of being thankful and appreciative for what you have in life, and it is driven primarily by *awareness*. Why awareness? Because it can be quite difficult to be thankful if you lack an honest awareness and recognition of your circumstances.

King Midas lacked awareness from the start, as he didn't understand or give any thought to all of the good things he already had in his life, most importantly his daughter. Instead, he obsessed over what he did *not* have. So rather than being grateful, he was driven almost to ruin by his greed.

Although it's a mythical fable, it is a theme that is all too common in the human experience. We fail to appreciate what we have, obsess over what we desire but do not possess, and struggle to be thankful for what really matters most.

Choosing Joy

Sometimes it takes a King Midas experience—losing everything—to appreciate what you have. In the case of Midas, the king lost everything because of his greed, but sometimes people lose everything through no fault of their own. This was the case for Anthony Ray Hinton, who spent thirty years on death row for crimes he did not commit.

In 1985, two fast food managers in Birmingham, Alabama were murdered in separate incidents, and Anthony was picked from a photo lineup by one of the survivors.

However, Anthony had a solid alibi; he worked at a supermarket warehouse and his boss confirmed that he was at work when both crimes were committed. Unfortunately, the jury ignored this testimony, and despite a lack of fingerprints or any other evidence connecting him to the crime scenes, Anthony was convicted of both murders and sentenced to death.

While imprisoned, he spent most of his time in solitary confinement, locked inside a five-by-seven-foot cell all alone. He was only allowed outside for one hour a day. Under such bitter and unfair circumstances, most people would have become angry, combative, and violent—and understandably so—but Anthony Hinton chose a different path. He quickly befriended many of the death row guards, some of whom would beg Anthony's attorney to get him out.

It took a long series of appeals, but eventually Anthony's case went before the Supreme Court of the United States.

The justices unanimously vacated the state court's conviction, ruling that Anthony's defense had been "constitutionally deficient." After that, the dominos quickly fell. The Alabama Court of Appeals closed his case, the Jefferson County district attorney dropped the case, and finally, on April 3, 2015, Anthony Hinton was released from prison.

After twenty-eight years on death row, Anthony Hinton was a free man. Afterward, he said, "One does not know the value of freedom until it is taken away. People run out of the rain. I run into the rain...I am so grateful for every drop. Just to feel it on my face."[8]

Rarely are people grateful for the feeling of rain on their faces, but when you are unjustly denied this simple sensation for twenty-eight years, suddenly it becomes a treasured experience.

As Anthony explained, "The world didn't give you your joy, and the world can't take it away. You can let people come into your life and destroy it, but I refuse to let anyone take

---

[8] Quoted in Dalai Lama and Desmond Tutu, *The Book of Joy* (New York: Avery, 2016).

my joy. I wake up in the morning and I don't need anyone to make me laugh. I'm going to laugh on my own because I have been blessed to see another day, and when you're blessed to see another day that should automatically give you joy."[9]

This is the power of gratitude. When you maintain awareness about what you have in your life, rather than focusing on what you don't have, you can embrace gratitude and find joy in almost any situation. This kind of awareness opens our senses and enables us to be attuned to everything that is around us. It is best manifested through slowing down, looking up, and being cognizant of what we have, often right in front of us.

As self-help author Melody Beattie said, "Gratitude turns what we have into enough, and more. It turns denial into acceptance, chaos into order, confusion into clarity...It makes sense of our past, brings peace for today, and creates a vision for tomorrow."[10]

---

[9] See *The Sun Does Shine: How I Found Life and Freedom on Death Row* (New York: St. Martin's Press, 2018), by Anthony Ray Hinton with Lara Love Hardin.

[10] https://melodybeattie.com/gratitude-2/

The Path of Gratitude

So how does awareness-driven gratitude move us closer to lasting peace and joy?

1. *Gratitude Shines a Light on the Positive*

Gratitude is the gift that helps you recognize and affirm the good and positive things around you so you don't expend all of your thoughts and emotional energy on the things you lack. Anthony Hinton could have become a broken, embittered man, but he left death row able to appreciate the simplicity of the rainfall on his face.

A gratitude that is driven by awareness exposes our senses so that we may see wonderful things that we previously failed to notice. When that happens, we are able to view our lives, the world, and nature very differently. Suddenly, we realize that there is beauty everywhere. There is something positive to experience and find in almost every circumstance because of the light that gratitude shines on the overlooked.

At the river's edge, King Midas realized all of the beautiful things in his life that he'd already possessed long before he acquired the golden curse. This kind of awareness brings us closer to peace and joy as we notice the beauty that is already all around us. Sometimes it takes a life-changing experience to open our eyes to what we have, though the catalyst needn't be so dramatic.

Seeing and emphasizing the positive is a hallmark of gratitude. By doing so, we allow ourselves to be more optimistic and hopeful and, by extension, full of potential for peace and joy. It's this optimistic outlook that moves us closer to a genuine and sincere appreciation.

2. *Gratitude Reinforces Our Sense of Perspective*

Gratitude makes us more in tune with the things we should be thankful for, helping us to focus on what we have instead of what we don't have. Developing that perspective is essential for attaining peace and joy. Remember, peace and joy are less about *doing* and more about *being*. In this case, it's a matter of perspective: be mindful and aware of the good you have and the good in the world around you to find the harmony and balance of peace.

The Greek Stoic philosopher Epictetus put it this way: "He is a wise man who does not grieve for the things which he has not but rejoices for those which he has." Or as the journalist German Kent wrote, "It's a funny thing about life, once you begin to take note of the things you are grateful for, you begin to lose sight of the things that you lack."

It's particularly impactful to *remember when you wanted what you have now*. Think about that. We often forget too easily that the things we have now were what we once longed for. By calling this to mind, we gain a sense of perspective that will ground us in gratitude, serving as a reminder that we should be appreciative for all that we have and not fixate on what else we desire. In short, try approaching a situation from a mindset of abundance— that is to say, *knowing* you already have enough.

3. Gratitude Simplifies Things

Gratitude takes complicated and difficult situations and makes them more manageable by distilling what matters most, simplifying circumstances into their most practical and useful elements. Most people would step outside on a rainy day and think of all the inconveniences caused by the storm, much less delight in the experience by simply being grateful for the feeling of raindrops on their face.

Here's another example of perhaps the simplest human exchange: hello and goodbye. Often, they are casual and perfunctory, and even more often, they are taken for granted. Instead, try *holding* them, which is to say, pause to appreciate both the greeting and farewell. Consider whom you are with and be grateful for that time, that moment, for we sadly never know if and when it might be our last. Make it count, and by doing so, you'll have a richer respect for that gift and treasure it so much more.

By focusing on the moment, the emphasis becomes what remains in our lives right now. It clarifies the most complicated circumstances, revealing what truly matters and reducing our worries to their minimum, many of which are petty concerns. The simplification that occurs through gratitude is a profound experience that lightens our load and the weight of expectation that we often carry.

In the words of journalist Susan L. Taylor, "Gratitude makes everything that we have more than enough."

The Way to Awareness

In order to be grateful, you have to develop an awareness of the good that's all around you. So what are some ways to do this?

1. Be Present in the Moment

A popular refrain these days is *"Be present."* Too often, people are entirely focused on the past (what they had) or the future (what they want to have) at the expense of the present (what they have now). But dwelling on the past creates regret, and fixating on the future produces anxiety. Allow yourself to be present in the current moment and accept that this moment *right now* is a gift that allows you to eliminate thoughts about what's already happened or what's going to happen.

Consider *this* moment to be the only moment that matters. How do you do that? Stop. Look around. Take a deep breath. Hold a smile. Be still.

It's similar to how you may deal with stress. Recognize it and take a moment to name or identify it. Maybe it's something beautiful in nature. Maybe it's something good in your personal life. Allow it in. Focus on that good thing in the current moment and nothing else. Doing this makes the "goodness" more tangible and real. It takes a quiet mind to be present in the moment, but when you are, the result can be both heartfelt and worthwhile.

2. For Me, Not to Me

There's a mindset change that can have a dramatic effect on the way you deal with circumstances. Whatever happens in your life, see it as something happening *for* you rather than something happening *to* you. In other words, see it as bringing value into your life. What is the good that the universe is handing to you in every situation? If you can get there—even if you can only get there *sometimes*—you will find yourself in a more peaceful and joyful state.

Is it really possible to be grateful in every circumstance? Yes, but only if you're willing to be grateful for everything in your life no matter how good or bad you perceive it to be. From minor obstacles to the most significant challenges, be grateful for it all. That means being willing to trust that things happen for a reason and can work out as they're supposed to.

This is not to be viewed as a fatalist philosophy but instead a deeper understanding that not only are we able to handle what happens to us, but there is often an underlying gift that will ultimately be found. "For me, not to me" releases the need for controlling each event in our lives so we can instead allow for events to unfold as they're meant to.

3. Practice Makes Better

There's a problem with the phrase "Practice makes perfect." Chiefly, there's really no such thing as "perfect." However, gratitude is something you can get better at by practicing awareness. There's no complicated ritual required; you can incorporate some simple gratitude exercise into your life that works for you. For example, maybe you start the day by noting the things you appreciate, or perhaps you sit down in the evening with a journal and write down the things that happened that day that you're grateful for.

Find a routine that works for you and fits easily into your life and try to stick with it. Regularly seeing the things that you should be grateful for will build your "gratitude muscle" over time. You'll become more aware of the good things in your life, and your perspective about your current circumstances and life will gradually change.

There is no right way to do this; the only wrong way would be not to do it at all. Practicing gratitude can become a powerful exercise of appreciation that keeps you rooted in the moment and leads you further toward peace and joy.

An Effortless Principle

Of the five principles discussed in this book, gratitude is likely the easiest one to get started with. All it requires is a willingness to see and notice the good things that you already have in your life and in the world around you *right now*. This takes very little effort. Just open your eyes and see. Find *something* to be grateful for at this very moment.

As soon as you start looking at the good things in your life, suddenly you will notice an abundance of other things that you hadn't fully appreciated, which will then cause you to cherish them in a more thankful way. The simplicity of nature's beauty can be enough. There are so many things to notice and appreciate; you only have to be willing to see them.

Gratitude makes us more optimistic about life, the world, and even the future because we're willing to look for and find the good in everything everywhere. It's not that we're naive or unaware of difficulties, tragedies, and suffering. We're not burying our heads in the sand. Rather, we are simply learning to recognize and appreciate good things in every situation that we might otherwise overlook.

Anthony Hinton's story captures this spirit of gratitude so beautifully, though it's important to note that he didn't ignore the fact that he had been unjustly imprisoned. On the contrary, he continued to work tirelessly to overturn the injustice and get released from death row.

However, even when wrongly imprisoned, we see in his story a man who tried every day to focus on the good things. Once he was released, he could have lived with regret and resentment, but he chose to focus on simple pleasures. He did not ignore the tragedy of his life; rather, he decided not to dwell on how he was wronged and instead take notice of the good that he now had. Anthony sees each new day as a gift in its purest and simplest form.

Many, if not everyone, has suffered loss in their lives. Some in very tragic and painful ways. No one should ever suggest that you mustn't feel sad for people or things that you've lost. However, grief and regret can consume our hearts and minds, and when we focus on what we've lost, we can forget what we have left. Under these circumstances, being grateful is certainly easier said than done. But gratitude can help shift our focus and in some ways becomes a much-needed interruption and therapy from hardship and sadness.

When we're more optimistic, we learn to love our circumstances without any terms or conditions. We don't live with the tension that robs so many people of happiness, a strain that says, "If only I had *this* or *that*, I would finally be happy." As we strengthen the gratitude muscle, we can eventually learn to have an unconditional love for life. When you get to that place, there's a real power in it, a power that cannot be taken from you.

Focus your energy and attention on the good that you have

right now. Don't waste time dwelling on what you lack, what others have that you do not, or what you've lost. Open your eyes to the abundance of gifts, blessings, and good things. Chances are, you already possess a lot more than you realize. Just be willing to see it all and be grateful for it.

Willing to See the Good

The story goes that there was once a young visually impaired woman who hated herself and her life simply because of her inability to see. Bitter, she pushed away almost everyone in her life, but she did have a boyfriend who loved her and stayed by her side through everything. He was always there for her, no matter what.

One day, in her bitterness, she told him, "If only I could see the world, I would marry you."

Not long after that, an anonymous benefactor donated a pair of eyes to her. She had them surgically implanted, and suddenly she could see everything around her—including her boyfriend.

Her loving boyfriend said, "Now that you can see the world, will you marry me?"

However, the woman was shocked to discover that her boyfriend was blind, too, so she refused to marry him. In tears, her boyfriend wrote a short note, handed it to her, and walked out of her life.

The woman opened the note and read it:

"Just take care of my eyes, dear."

So much human pain and sorrow are the result of failing to see the good that is right around us until it's too late. If you simply embrace awareness and begin to recognize the good and positive, rather than focusing on the negative, you will notice a difference in the quality of your life right away. Indeed, this is one of the most direct routes to peace and joy.

Through gratitude, we clarify what matters, and that, in turn, is how we develop our own sense of *integrity*, which we'll talk about next.

"Wear gratitude like a cloak, and it will
feed every corner of your life."

—RUMI

Chapter Three

Integrity

"Integrity has no need of rules."

—Albert Camus

A small boy and his father were fishing one night on the lake before bass fishing season officially opened. It had been an uneventful trip, but suddenly, the boy felt a strong pull on his fishing rod. He struggled to reel it in, but after a mighty tussle, he discovered that he'd caught the largest fish he'd ever seen in his young life.

"Wow, Dad, this fish must weigh at least fifteen pounds," the boy said, struggling to hold it in his arms.

"Good job, son," his father said, "but that's a largemouth bass."

Bass fishing season didn't technically start until the next day, so by law they were supposed to throw it back. The boy and his father glanced at each other. Then the father looked at his watch.

"It's ten o'clock at night," he said. "Bass season doesn't open for another two hours. I'm afraid we're going to have to throw it back in the water."

"But, Dad," the boy cried, "it's only two more hours! Can't we keep it anyway? We'll never catch a fish as big as this one again!"

"There will be others," his father said. "It's more important to do the right thing."

The boy looked around the lake. He saw no other boats and no other fishermen anywhere nearby. Then he turned to his father again.

"We're all alone on the lake right now," he said. "If we keep the fish, no one will ever know except for us."

But his father held his ground. "But *we'll* know. Doing the right thing is not just about other people," he said. "It's about *us*."

The decision was not negotiable, so the boy was forced to unhook the enormous bass and toss it back into the lake.

Many years later, as an adult, he reflected on that moment with his father.

"We never did catch a fish that big ever again," he said. "But I've seen that same fish many more times in my life—whenever there's a question or issue about *integrity*."

Yes, our third foundational principle is integrity, which has two significant definitions, both of which are helpful for our discussion in this book: "adherence to moral and ethical principles; soundness of moral character" and "the state of being whole, entire, or undiminished."[11]

Integrity and Decency

The fuel that drives integrity is *decency*, which means setting a standard of right and wrong and then conforming to that standard with consistency. Decent people are honest and have clear, measurable moral principles and personal ethics that they adhere to, which gives them a sense of respectability and trustworthiness. Reliable, with a dignity that's intact, they keep their word regardless of whether or not it's convenient to do so.

---

[11] https://www.dictionary.com/browse/integrity

If we are decent people who truly possess integrity, then we'll live by our moral code whether no one is watching or everyone is watching. Those with integrity wear that badge unassumingly, with a sense of being that is nonnegotiable. Former United States Senator Alan K. Simpson appropriately affirmed, "If you have integrity, nothing else matters. If you don't have integrity, nothing else matters."

By extension, dignity and *correctness* are not just ambiguous ideals without any purpose. They mean something. Consider the alternative and you'll appreciate how essential it is for you—for all of us—to uphold our basic responsibility as human beings. Integrity that elicits decency creates the nucleus for who we are at our core. When it counts—and when it doesn't—who are you? But, of course, it *always* counts.

The Good Seed

Although the following story has been told in many different forms, it's basic lesson on integrity is timeless no matter the version.

Once upon a time, there was an emperor who had no children and needed to choose a successor. Thousands of children from across the kingdom came to the palace and were surprised when the emperor exclaimed that he was going to choose one of them as his heir.

He gave each of the children a single seed and instructed them to return home to their villages, where they were to plant their seed in a pot and tend to it for a year. When they returned after the year was up, the emperor would judge their efforts of maintaining the plant and choose his successor accordingly.

Among the children, there was a boy named Ling who received his seed and returned to his village in haste. His mother helped him choose a pot, put some soil in it, and bury the seed. Ling tended to his potted plant and watered it carefully every day.

Once a week, the children of the village would get together to compare their plants. After a couple of weeks, there were signs of life in all but Ling's pot. The weeks passed and Ling continued to water his pot every day, but no plant grew.

After a few months, many of the plants really began to blossom. Some children had trees growing in their pots, some had flowers, and some had leafy shrubs. But poor Ling still had nothing growing in his pot. The other children began making fun of him; nevertheless, Ling continued to water his pot every day.

A year passed, and finally it was time to return to the palace to show the emperor what had grown in each pot so he could select his heir. Ling was anxious because his pot had never shown any signs of life.

"I can't return to the palace with this empty pot," Ling said. "They won't know I've watered it every day. They will accuse me of being lazy! What if they punish me?"

His mother looked him in the eye and said, "Son, whatever the consequences are, you must return to the emperor and show him your empty pot."

Even though he was scared, Ling returned to the palace with the other children and entered through the front gates. By now, some of the plants that the children had grown looked magnificent, and the children were excited to discover which one the emperor would choose.

The emperor came out of the palace and made his way through the crowd, looking at the many impressive trees, shrubs, and flowers that were on display. Some of the children puffed their chests out and tried to look as regal as possible, hoping that they would be chosen as the heir to the empire.

Then the emperor came to Ling. He looked at the empty pot. Then he looked at Ling.

"What happened here?" he asked. "You have nothing but dirt in your pot."

"Sir, I watered my pot every day, but nothing ever grew," Ling muttered, nervous and embarrassed.

The emperor moved on. After a few hours, he finished his assessment, looking at all of the wonderful plants. Finally, he stood in front of the children and congratulated them on their efforts.

"It is clear to me that some of you desperately want to be emperor and would do anything to make that happen," he said. "But there is one boy that I would like to point out, for he has come to me with nothing. Ling, please approach."

Oh, no, Ling thought. *Now I'm going to be punished.*

He trudged to the front of the group, clutching his barren pot in his arms. When he got there, the emperor took the pot from him and held it aloft for all to see. The other children laughed.

Then the emperor said, "One year ago, I gave each of you a seed. I told you to return home, plant the seed, and bring back your plant. But here is the secret: The seeds I gave to each of you were boiled until they were no longer viable and wouldn't grow. Yet somehow, I see before me thousands of plants and only one barren pot. You have all cheated, except for Ling. Since integrity and courage are more important values for leadership than a proud display, Ling will be my heir."

The Path of Integrity

So how does decency-driven integrity guide us toward lasting peace and joy?

1. *Integrity Makes Us Solid*

Having a set of personal ethics that you live by makes you whole by providing a solid basis for being. As Frederick Douglass said, "I prefer to be true to myself, even at the hazard of incurring the ridicule of others, rather than to be false, and to incur my own abhorrence."

When you know what you believe and live according to those beliefs, you have the foundation and confidence to not only make decisions but to feel *right* about them. This contributes greatly to peace and joy because you are free from internal division, self-judgment, or cognitive dissonance. You don't dwell on inconsistent beliefs or rationalize poor decisions but rather, maintain an inner strength that defines your being as true and intact.

The beauty of integrity is that it allows you to define your identity. Who are you? What do you stand for? Why does your word mean anything? The answers to these questions are unequivocal when you have integrity.

2. *Integrity Becomes Our Default*

The businessman Henry Kravis said, "If you don't have integrity, you have nothing. You can't buy it. You can have all the money in the world, but if you are not a moral and ethical person, you really have nothing." What does he mean by this? Simply that integrity provides a moral reference point for decision making, which helps you eliminate gray areas in your behavior so you can feel good about the things you do and how you conduct yourself.

A key element to this is the elimination of rationalization. When we have integrity and thus a moral reference point, there's no need to try to justify or rationalize a decision that is not in alignment with our personal ethics. Too often, we try to defend certain positions despite knowing that we are in the wrong. With integrity, we stay true to what we know is right as well as to ourselves. Having that default brings us a sense of peace, knowing that there is a basis for our choices.

3. Integrity Provides a Soft Pillow

According to an old proverb, "There is no pillow as soft as a clear conscience." You can't have a clear conscience without a clear sense of right and wrong. When you live in such a way that you do what you believe to be right, regardless of whether people are watching or not, then you will live with a profound sense of lightness in your mind and heart.

Storyteller Brené Brown wrote, "Integrity is choosing courage over comfort; choosing what is right over what is fun, fast, or easy; and choosing to practice our values rather than simply professing them." No, it's not always fun, fast, or easy to be a decent person who lives by what they think is right, but you'll sleep easier at night because you'll feel better about who you are—knowing you did right.

Peace is one of the two chief aims of this book; it is perhaps best epitomized by this aspect of integrity. After all, how can we find peace with anything but a clear conscience? Integrity provides this inner balance and harmony.

The Way to Decency

When we're talking about living with integrity, we're really talking about being a decent person. So what does it take to embody decency?

1. Define Your Values

This is perhaps the most obvious starting place. You can't live according to a set of morals and ethics if you don't have one. Figure out what *you* mean when you think of "right and wrong." Bear in mind, this isn't just about figuring out *what* you stand for but *why* you stand for it as well.

Also remember, this is about identifying the values that *you* will live by, not values that you will attempt to impose on others. It's about feeling solid *in yourself*, so be respectful toward others and the foundation they might've set for themselves.

Sometimes, living according to our own morals requires us to make some decisions that don't make sense to others. Jon Huntsman Sr. was the founder and CEO of Huntsman

Chemical Corporation. According to a story he recounts in his book *Barefoot to Billionaire*, he made an agreement with Emerson Kampen, the CEO of Great Lakes Chemical Company, to sell 40 percent of his company for $54 million. Jon sealed the deal with a handshake, as he liked to do.

However, months later, when it was time to sign the paperwork for the agreement, the price of raw materials had plummeted, and Huntsman's profits had risen. Emerson called Jon and said, "According to our bankers, 40 percent of your company is now worth $250 million. Given the circumstances, we no longer believe it's fair for us to pay you just $54 million. It's not enough. Although we can't pay the full $250 million, we'd like to offer $100 million. That's more than our original agreement, but it seems like the right thing to do."

However, Jon replied, "We agreed to a price of $54 million, and that's the price I expect you to pay. We already shook on it."

"It's not fair to you, Jon," Emerson replied.

"I'll tell you what," Jon Huntsman said, "you negotiate for yourself, and I'll negotiate for me."[12]

In the end, the sale went through at $54 million.

Now why would Jon do that? Why would he negotiate himself out of another $46 million? Because having integrity means sticking to your principles and keeping your word, and the bond of that handshake agreement was more important to him than additional profits. As Jon knew, being a decent person will always contribute far more to your sense of peace and joy than trying to gain as much as you can in any situation.

2. Take Responsibility

In order to have integrity, you have to be completely honest with yourself. That means taking responsibility for your actions. Once you've defined your values, then you know who you want to be deep down. Be honest with yourself

---

[12] Jon Hunstman, *Barefoot to Billionaire: Reflections on a Life's Work and a Promise to Cure Cancer* (New York: Abrams, 2014).

about how you're living up to that self-image and always try to reside in that place of decency.

The simplest and most important way that you embody a life of integrity and decency is by keeping your word. Do what you say you'll do. Not only does this make other people think more highly of you, but it helps you to think more highly of yourself. Make the decision that your word is your bond, and you will begin to see a transformation in your life.

Indeed, it will set you apart from the pack. Those who know you will reflect on this and say, "That person always does what they say they're going to do. You can always count on them." And when people can truly say that about you—and when you can say that about yourself—then you know you have embodied a key element of integrity. In today's day and age, you'll be as rare and magical as a unicorn.

3. Keep the Right Company

If you want to live with integrity, it helps to keep company with other people who have integrity. This doesn't mean surrounding yourself with self-righteous people—that won't do you much good, especially since we're also trying to avoid judgment. Rather, it's about finding people who have clearly defined values and trying to live by them consistently.

It's been said that we are a combination of our five closest friends. In many ways, the people we choose to associate with says more about us and the kind of person we're striving to be. In fact, spending time with people who have integrity will inspire you to have it as well. The presence of those who understand and appreciate its virtue instills a certain responsibility in us, and in many ways, being around those with integrity can provide a sense of accountability. Ultimately, there is much to be gained by paying close attention to the people you align yourself with.

Satisfy the Soul

Lessons on integrity can be taught by people of all ages, sometimes in simple yet profound ways. Consider the following story.

Once upon a time, there was a boy who had a great collection of marbles and a girl who had a great selection of sweets. They looked at each other's possessions and felt mutual envy. So they agreed on an exchange.

"I'll give you all of my marbles," the boy said, "and you give me all of your sweets."

They made the trade. However, the boy secretly kept his biggest and best marble, giving the rest of them to the girl, but the girl gave all of her sweets to the boy, just as she had promised.

That night, when the girl lay down in bed, she drifted off into a pleasant sleep, while the boy tossed and turned, wondering if the girl had hidden some of her sweets from him, just as he'd hidden his best marble from her.

Returning to our soft pillow analogy, integrity is the solution to the internal conflict that plagues so many people and causes so many sleepless nights. Our conscience knows when we make a choice or decision that is not in alignment with our principles. There's nowhere to hide when we know deep down the difference between right and wrong.

In order to feel lasting peace and joy, we first need to feel solid. That's where integrity comes in, providing a strong, consistent core for all of our decision making. If you haven't already done so, take some time to define a clear and consistent code of morals and ethics for yourself, then make that code the compass of your entire life.

As Maya Angelou said, "Just do right. Right may not be expedient or profitable, but it will satisfy the soul."

Eliminating the gray areas in your decision making brings you closer to real peace and joy in your life. Unburdened by self-contradicting behavior, you will feel lighter and less burdened, and that, in turn, will help you embody our next foundational principle: humility.

*"Integrity is making sure
that the things you say and the things
you do are in alignment."*

—KATRINA MAYER

Chapter Four

Humility

*"Humility is not thinking less of yourself;
it's thinking of yourself less."*

—C. S. LEWIS

I n the simple words of Confucius, "Humility is the solid foundation of all virtues." An equally simple tale about George Washington demonstrates why this is so.

As the story goes, George Washington was out riding on horseback near what was then called District of Columbia with a group of friends. They crossed a broad farmer's field and approached a low stone wall. To get to a road on the other side, they had to jump their horses over the wall. In the process, one of the horses kicked the wall with his back hooves and knocked a number of the stones loose, which tumbled to the ground.

"We'd better replace those stones," Washington said, reining in his horse.

"Oh, let the farmer who owns this land take care of them," one of the friends replied. "Such a menial task is below your station."

At the time, Washington listened to his friend and rode on, leaving the tumbled stones on the ground. However, it didn't sit right with him. When the riding party was over, he decided to return and repair the wall.

Accompanied by a riding companion, he rode back the way they'd come until he found the same spot on the wall. Then he dismounted and went to work carefully replacing each of the stones. His riding companion saw what he was doing and remarked, "Mr. President, you're far too big to be doing a job like that."

"On the contrary," Washington replied, "I am just the right size."

Humility and Perspective

Nearly two hundred years later, another distinguished statesman exemplified the virtue of humility in an even more personal way. Sam Rayburn served twenty-four terms as a United States congressman from 1913 to 1961 for Texas's Fourth Congressional District, including seventeen years as Speaker of the House of Representatives. During his time as Speaker, Rayburn wielded tremendous power and prestige, and he was third in the line of succession for the presidency.

One day, he learned that the teenage daughter of a reporter friend had tragically died, so early the next morning, he went to the friend's house to pay him a visit. He knocked on the door and when the friend opened it, Sam said, "I've heard the terrible news. I'm so sorry for your loss, my friend. Is there anything I can do to help?"

His friend stammered for a moment before replying, "No, Mr. Speaker, I don't think there's anything you can do. We are making all of the funeral arrangements today."

"Well, it's still early," Sam said. "Have you had your morning coffee yet?"

"No, I haven't had time to make it," the grieving man replied.

"In that case," said Sam, "please allow me to make the coffee for you."

The friend invited him in, and Sam proceeded to make a pot of coffee. As the friend watched Sam Rayburn, one of the most powerful men in the country, making him coffee, he suddenly remembered something.

"Mr. Speaker, weren't you supposed to have breakfast at the White House this morning?"

"Yes, I was," Sam replied, "but I called the President and told him I couldn't come because I had a friend in need."

These stories capture the essence of humility, which is generally defined as, "having a modest opinion or estimate of one's own importance that is free from pride or arrogance."

At its heart, humility is about having a *perspective* that is clear and sensible about our own importance. Although we often connect this quality with modesty, at its core is a genuine recognition that we are all the same—we're all just human beings. Understanding this creates a clearer lens and valuable check as to one's personal significance.

We are then able to acknowledge our limitations, which in turn can open our minds to cultivating each of the other principles, as they all connect directly to the often-neglected virtue of humility.

The Path of Humility

So how does perspective-driven humility contribute to lasting peace and joy?

1. Humility Eases the Weight of Self-Importance

An inflated sense of self-importance contributes to a feeling of entitlement, which can make even minor frustrations seem like enormous burdens. When we remove that weight, it eases our minds by helping us let go of that inflated ego so we are no longer prisoners of our own privilege.

Our pride can often get in the way of understanding and appreciating that we are fallible and imperfect. Humility allows for more realistic, reasonable expectations, which promotes a spirit that is light and free. By recognizing this effect, much of our burden is lifted, paving the way to a more peaceful sense of being. This can feel like *relief*, as we are able to resist the need and desire to think more of ourselves.

2. *Humility Soothes the Soul*

Humility alters the way we view our circumstances so that we see things for what they are in the grand scheme of things. With this broader perspective, we are able to cut through self-preoccupation, seeing others as equals, which stimulates compassion and inspires our previous virtues: kindness and gratitude.

In a sense, humility is a through line that touches *all* of our foundational principles, because it gives us the proper lens to view each of them. When we are humble, we take ourselves out of the equation, enabling us to cope with worry and anxiety much more easily. "The universe is not all about me," we can say, "because I am just one person."

Our hardships and frustrations are no longer viewed as universal injustices; it can become soothing to be mindful of this truth, especially when we *know* and *believe* it to be true.

3. Humility Recenters Our Purpose

When we're humble, we gain a healthier focus on the things that really matter. Much of the internal noise and distraction is removed because we no longer need to be constantly obsessed with serving the self. Life becomes simpler, easier, and cleaner because, after all, what does it matter if everything doesn't go our way? We're just simple human beings, not divinities who deserve to have our every whim and sense of entitlement satisfied.

Many people go through life feeling weighed down and burdened, heavy with stress and troubles, but what they often fail to realize is that the heaviest burden they bear is their own entitled sense of need. That mindset is the way to ruin, and adopting a humble perspective on life will go a long way toward recentering our purpose and helping us understand what truly matters most.

Oftentimes, we find a sense of purpose or perspective *when* things don't go our way. To say we have been *humbled* by something or someone can be very grounding and a valuable experience. It's in this instance that we have the opportunity to see things differently and to see more clearly.

As psychologist Yasmin Mogahed put it, "Never curse a fall. The ground is where humility lives."

The Way to a Humble Perspective

How can we adopt a humble perspective of ourselves and embody this quality in our lives?

1. Cultivate Awe

Awe is a powerful emotion for seeing the wonder in life— and in other people. When we allow ourselves to be awe-struck by the world around us, we worry less about being awestruck by ourselves.

How many people are struggling because they have failed to achieve highly ambitious, self-imposed personal or professional goals? There's nothing wrong with working toward a goal, but humility permits us to stop trying to impress ourselves and others in order to find happiness. There are plenty of magnificent things around you right now. Allow yourself to be touched by them, no matter where you are with your goals.

An essential trait of humble people is a curiosity about the world and other people. They have an almost child-like interest in even simple things, such as conversations, events, interactions, moments of play, and ordinary beauty.

The benefits of cultivating awe—or what we might call the growth of wonder—can be both unexpected and extraordinary, allowing us to see many beautiful things that most people tend to overlook. More often than not, it's these little things that end up making a considerable difference in our journey toward peace and joy.

2. Be Situationally Aware

Situational awareness is a remarkable sign of emotional intelligence. We *notice* what's going on around us because we're not so wrapped up in ourselves that we become distracted or indifferent. How do you become situationally aware? Heighten your attention to notice what's happening *around* you during each moment. From the slightest activity to the most conspicuous movements, open your eyes and be mindful of them.

Only a humble man would notice that he'd knocked a few stones off a farmer's wall while out riding with friends, much less return to fix it. Only a humble man would notice that a grieving friend hadn't had the time to make his morning coffee, much less postpone an important meeting in order to make that coffee.

As part of developing situational awareness, notice your relative size and significance in the grand scheme of things. It's okay to admit that you're just one small being in a very big world. Don't be afraid to acknowledge your own relative insignificance in the universe. In fact, by admitting this, you will free yourself from the burdensome need for self-achievement that robs so many people of peace.

Having situational awareness enables us to recognize opportunities for compassion, inspiring us to appreciate small moments of beauty which contribute to our peace and joy. So open your eyes and see what's happening around you. Doing so will sharpen your senses, enhance your perceptiveness, and improve your decision making. But be warned: Situational awareness may require you to lift your head up from your smartphone from time to time, if only for a moment.

3. Listen Up

Author Meg Cabot said it quite well: "There is a difference between listening and hearing, just as there is a difference between seeing and knowing."

If we're humble, we will realize that we learn more from listening to others than we'll ever learn from listening only to ourselves. Humility makes us teachable because we admit that we don't know everything. This acknowledgment creates even greater opportunities for growth, development, and enlightenment.

But don't just *listen* to others. More importantly, learn to *hear well*. In practical terms, that means when we're having a conversation, we aren't just thinking about the next thing we want to say. We're not focused on preparing our response. Instead, we're trying to pay attention to what the other person is saying and understand what they mean. Not surprisingly, kindness and gratitude both come to us with greater ease when we make a conscious decision to listen *and hear*.

Peace Within

Humility is often underappreciated because there are those who worry it will compromise their confidence or self-esteem. Some even fear that humility will make them feel worthless. Author C. Joybell C. addressed this when she said, "Be careful not to mistake insecurity and inadequacy for humility. Humility has nothing to do with the insecure and inadequate. Just like arrogance has nothing to do with greatness."

The truth is, a healthy humility is about being at peace with ourselves because we are able to let go of inflated pride and any trace of arrogance. Humility is, in fact, a true source of strength. We see this in the lives of both George Washington and Sam Rayburn. They didn't feel like they were above doing acts of kindness that were "below their station." Free of the burden of ego, they were grounded, down to earth, and able to make an impact on those around them.

Carl Sagan wrote, "We are like butterflies who flutter for a day and think it is forever." To be sure, life is fragile and our place in it is very small. As of 2021, there are approximately eight billion people in the world, and scientific consensus says there have been somewhere around 117 billion humans born on the planet over the entire course of human history.[13]

Take that in. Don't be afraid of it. Individually, we are quite small, so why should we waste another drop of emotional energy trying to confirm our own importance?

That doesn't mean you're worthless. On the contrary, we are all unique and special beings, even if we're ephemeral and tiny. Yes, every human being who has ever lived, or will live, is unique and fleeting—and that fact is nothing to shy away from.

A Mark of Greatness

Take this one final anecdote from arguably the most famous physicist of all time.

---

[13] https://www.prb.org/articles/how-many-people-have-ever-lived-on-earth/

Shortly after he moved to America, Albert Einstein was invited to give an address before a group of mathematicians at Princeton University. It took some coaxing, as he claimed he had nothing to say that the audience didn't already know.

Finally, he agreed to speak on some aspects of tensor analysis, a tool essential to the mathematical treatment of relativity theory. A small card announcing the speaker, location, and time was hung on the notice board in Fine Hall, the venue for the event.

When the day for the address arrived, Princeton University campus was filled, overflowing with automobiles and a great crowd of people trying to get into the small auditorium.

As it turned out, the little card posted on the notice board in Fine Hall—and intended for only those few mathematicians who might be interested in the topic—was read by some students who then informed other students. Those students then wrote home to their parents, and their parents invited various friends and acquaintances to attend the event with them. Everyone wanted to hear the great man speak.

Einstein was led through the restless crowd and placed in a seat in the front row of the little auditorium to await his introduction at the proper moment. Swiveling his head, he looked about the room in surprise at the vast throng of people struggling to squeeze into the hall.

Seeing the large crowd, he exclaimed to those seated nearby, "I never realized that in America there was so much interest in tensor analysis."

It's a simple yet useful reminder about awareness—self-awareness, in fact—and humility. Free yourself from the burden of self-importance and embrace a perspective that sees the significance of events, small circumstances, and the people around you. Remove yourself from the equation and live with lightness. Cultivate awe in the world so you can enjoy all of the beautiful moments.

Nothing will contribute more to your feeling of lightness than embracing a more limited and modest view of your own importance. Minimize the ego in order to maximize the soul. When we're able to do that, it leads directly to our last foundational principle: acceptance.

"If you are humble nothing will touch you,
neither praise nor disgrace, because
you know what you are."

—MOTHER TERESA

Chapter Five

Acceptance

"Don't spend time beating on a wall,
hoping to transform it
into a door."

—Coco Chanel

A psychology professor stood before her class. A large glass of water sat on the table before her. She reached down and grabbed the glass, raising it above her head.

"Okay, class, how heavy is this glass of water I'm holding?" she asked.

Students began shouting out answers.

"A couple of ounces," one said.

"One pound," said another.

"Two pounds," said a third.

The professor waited until the students were done guessing. After fielding many answers, she finally shook her head and said, "The real answer is that the actual weight of the glass of water is irrelevant for determining its heaviness. In reality, its heaviness depends on how long I hold it. If I hold it for a minute, it will feel very light. If I hold it for an hour, it will be heavy enough to make my arm ache.

However, if I hold it for a full day without setting it down, it will become so heavy that my arm will likely cramp up, my hand will grow numb, and I will drop the glass onto the floor. In each case, the actual weight of the glass doesn't change, but the heaviness does."

The point was not lost on most of her students, who nodded thoughtfully.

The professor continued, "Your worries, frustrations, disappointments, and stressful thoughts are like this glass of water. Think about them for a little while and nothing drastic will happen. Think about them a little longer, and you will begin to feel a noticeable pain. Think about them all day long, and you will grow completely numb and paralyzed, unable to do anything else."

The Wolf We Feed

A similar story is told about a Native American grandfather who wanted to explain to his grandson about how he felt. "It is as if two wolves are fighting within my heart," he said.

"One wolf is vengeful, angry, and violent, but the other wolf is loving and compassionate."

At this, the grandson gasped and said, "But, Grandfather, which wolf will win the fight within your heart?"

The grandfather looked at this grandson gravely and said, "Whichever one I feed."

We make choices all the time about what we're going to hold on to and what we're going to let go of. To that end, our fifth and final foundational principle is *acceptance*.

The dictionary definition of acceptance is, "agreeing and consenting to receive something offered." However, for the purposes of this book, we're talking specifically about receiving the things that happen in your life, both the things you like and the things you don't like.

When something happens to us, we have the power to choose whether or not we accept it. One reason why so many people lack peace and joy is because they struggle to accept things that have happened in their lives—not just major tragedies but the small disappointments, heartbreaks, and frustrations that add up over time.

Acceptance is not easy because it requires us to look more closely at the role we've played in our own realities. It's much more convenient to view our circumstances as events that happened *to* us, but the truth can sometimes be inconvenient in that regard. Instead, when we accept what others have done—and acknowledge what we have done as well—we take a step forward in coming to terms with what *is*. This can become a significant breakthrough in personal growth, with the realization that what we do control is the wolf we're going to feed.

Acceptance and Flexibility

Acceptance is made easier through *flexibility*, which is the ability to cope with change and the willingness to endure the undesired. Flexibility is essential to acceptance because it helps us to understand that we cannot control each and every element of our existence.

It also gives us the ability to identify signs of change, thereby allowing us to adapt to the unfamiliar and uncomfortable.

By holding what are often conflicting feelings, we start to accept there are truths that we may or may not like and appreciate that they are beyond our control.

However, we can adapt to this conflict and change, which is a hallmark of flexibility and, by extension, an indication of secure and strong mental health. It's the ability to *flex* or bend to circumstances that stretches our capacity to accept things, *especially* when it's something that we do not like or want.

Although the dictionary definition of acceptance is fairly broad, we are going to distill our principle of acceptance into more practical terms. To be sure, it's easy to accept things that we *want*, though most of the time, we struggle to accept things that we don't want. Unhappiness is often the result of not wanting something but *getting it anyway.* That tension of opposites produces stress, anger, and many other negative emotions that rob us of peace and joy. With acceptance, we acknowledge that we may not want something but that we can have the emotional and mental flexibility to allow it with less resistance.

It should be noted that acceptance is not quite the same

as tolerating something, because tolerance might suggest *putting up with it*. On the contrary, when we accept something, it means we've come to terms with it and maybe even learned to embrace it. That doesn't necessarily mean that we think it's good. It's possible to recognize that something is bad and still be reconciled to its existence. In fact, that's a reality we need to embrace if we're going to find peace and joy.

The Path of Acceptance

So how does flexibility-driven acceptance help us achieve sustainable peace and joy?

1. Acceptance Grounds You in What Is

Brazilian novelist Paulo Coelho put it this way: "It's best to accept life as it really is and not as I imagined it to be."

Acceptance grounds you in what *is* rather than what *isn't* so you can acknowledge and address the truth. After all, we'll never achieve sustainable peace and joy if we can't deal with reality.

By rooting ourselves in reality and accepting what *is*, we don't have to live in denial or self-delusion. Consequently, we are able to see our problems for what they are and consider our actual options for dealing with them. This includes owning 100 percent of what you bring to a situation, which is critical when confronting reality, especially as it relates to your contribution to it. In taking personal responsibility, you become even more deeply grounded in what is.

Acceptance then allows us to make better decisions that are more relevant to our real circumstances because we're not afraid to see things as they are. By extension, our peace and joy exist in the real world, not in some imaginary place created in our mind through denial.

Being grounded in what *is* activates resilience, which is the capacity to both accept challenges and *absorb* them. In learning to accept circumstances rather than trying to dismiss them, we create a path forward for an even greater strength.

2. *Acceptance Helps Us Let Go*

Acceptance releases us from the need for control, freeing us from the burden—and illusion—of believing that we may always direct events toward the exact outcome we desire. Letting go removes a considerable psychological weight, allowing us to find a peace and joy that are disconnected from our desire to control our circumstances, ultimately creating a firm and solid foundation.

As the author Joanne Harris wrote, "After a while, whoever you are, you just have to let go, and the river brings you home."[14] Further, it's been said that in the end, what matters most is how well you lived, how well you loved, and how well you learned to let go. It's the last that will enable you to live and love so much better.

By letting go of the need for control, we let go of the fear. That's what really drives the demand for control, after all, so releasing that compulsion helps remove the burden. And from that comes a newfound confidence in knowing that you can handle the reality of your circumstances—without having to control them.

---

[14] See *Five Quarters of the Orange: A Novel* (New York: Harper Perennial, 2007).

3. Acceptance Provides for Realistic Expectations

One of life's great frustrations is expecting things that can never come to pass. Acceptance instead helps us to focus on those outcomes that are realistic and likely to occur. This doesn't mean we shouldn't continue to dream big, but it does free us from the burden of expecting to receive what we may never have.

Acceptance gets to the heart of—and eliminates—the need to worry, an emotion that doesn't serve any valuable purpose and will always be futile. Sociologist Karl Pillemer's book *30 Lessons for Living* details his findings from conversations with over a thousand older Americans. Over the course of these conversations, they shared what they had learned about living well. In his conclusion, Pillemer writes, "Those at the end of their lives, when looking back, were able to reflect on the one thing they regretted—it was the worrying."

Having realistic expectations helps to assuage the everyday concerns that we allow to consume us, concerns that don't offer any practical utility. In accepting them for what they are (usually of little importance), we can devote our energy to more sustaining and rewarding endeavors.

The Trouble with Dandelions

There was a man who took great pride in his lawn. One day, he discovered that a large crop of dandelions had sprung up there, so he set out to eliminate them. He mowed the lawn, but the dandelions soon grew back. He picked them by hand, but they still returned. He tried a range of lawn care products, but the dandelions just wouldn't stop growing in his lawn.

Finally, he wrote a letter to the US Department of Agriculture.

Dear Sir or Madam,

My beautiful lawn is infested with dandelions. I have tried everything I can think of to get rid of them, but they keep coming back. Right now, my front yard is filled with these yellow flowers. What shall I do now?

He put his letter in the mail and waited for a response. A week later, he received a reply from the Department of Agriculture. Opening the envelope, he pulled out a very brief letter with an official US government letterhead at the top.

Dear Sir,

We suggest you learn to love them.

The Way to Flexibility

How can we embrace acceptance and use flexibility to learn to deal with life as it is?

1. Feel It First

In order to learn to accept something, you first have to recognize and acknowledge how you really feel about it— and why you feel that way. Only being truthful about how you feel allows you to move forward and learn to accept what is. Remember, a key part of "what is" includes "how you really feel." Acceptance relative to our emotions is essential for being able to admit what are sometimes difficult feelings.

Vulnerability emerges once again, as it is a key element in taking stock of *why* you feel that way. It's the *why* that helps you let go of whatever you may be holding on to and compels you to come to terms with your reality.

Although this may not come naturally for many of us, "feeling it first" compels you to take a significant step toward developing the tool of flexibility, providing the basis for what's real—and real for you. Coming to terms with these feelings clears the path for even greater growth to overcome our own internal emotional obstacles.

2. Eliminate Ego

Acceptance goes hand in hand with our previous virtue, humility. One of the easiest ways to humble yourself is to honestly assess and accept your own significance in the grand scheme of things. This helps to eliminate ego, which is important because an inflated sense of importance tends to make undesired events even more frustrating. We think, "Why should this happen to *me*?"

We've all struggled with these kinds of ego-driven thoughts. Instead, accept and concede that not everything will go your way. Eliminating ego allows us to look at circumstances, including the decisions of others, objectively, from the outside. By doing so, you can reasonably assess situations as if you were a stranger, with no agenda or stake in the outcome, which can then help you respond with clarity.

As Ryan Holiday writes in *Ego Is the Enemy*, "Most of us aren't 'egomaniacs,' but ego is there at the root of almost every conceivable problem and obstacle, from why we can't win to why we need to win all the time and at the expense of others. From why we don't have what we want to why having what we want doesn't seem to make us feel any better."[15]

3. Find the Positive to Make Peace

An effective way of learning acceptance is to look for the positive in every situation. With the right perspective and a bit of objectivity, you can find some positive even in a negative outcome. Maybe it taught you an important lesson

---

[15] *Ego is the Enemy* (New York: Penguin, 2016).

or brought someone important into your life. Perhaps it showed you a better way forward or simply made you stronger. More than that, trying to find the positive helps you to accept each circumstance and condition so you can see the sunshine even on the cloudiest of days.

Finding the positive allows you to take steps toward ultimately making peace with your situation. You've acknowledged the reality and come to terms with the things that are not in your control. By honestly assessing the situation and finding something positive to take from it, you can now make peace with it. This might take time, even an entire lifetime, but by finding the positive, you set yourself on the path toward peace.

The concept of the journey is prevalent in this idea, as for many of us, this path is far from straight or linear. Rather, it's a winding road and one in which we may bend but not entirely break. But having gone through such a process makes us stronger, creating a powerful vulnerability that fosters a newfound enlightenment.

In the words of Deepak Chopra, "Nothing brings down walls as surely as acceptance."

Life Is What You Make It

Acceptance is not giving in; it is acknowledging the truth. With acceptance, we are no longer feeding emotions that don't serve us in any constructive or useful way. We don't have to hold on to feelings of being wronged, upset, hurt, or angry. We let them go by accepting that we cannot control them—we can only control how we feel about them.

This doesn't mean we have to condone acts that caused pain. It simply means that we've made peace with them in an effort to realize our own sense of peace. Doing this clears out our inner clutter and creates space for joy. With acceptance, we may have conflicted feelings about something that has happened, even as we accept that it *has* happened. That's okay. It stretches our flexibility when we accept that we can't have everything in life exactly as we wish.

As a result, we find patience and a clearer mind, body, and soul. You've perhaps heard the saying, "You live most of your life inside your head, so make sure it's a nice place to be." Problems are a part of life. Only when we are no longer alive will we be free of trouble, so learning to accept life as it comes, especially those things we can't control, defuses our problems so they do not hold mastery over us.

What we learn to accept, we stand to conquer.

Now, bear in mind, this principle may require some effort on your part. Indeed, all of these virtues may require some effort. However, there are no complicated processes that have to be introduced into your daily routine, though you may have to consciously work on embodying them. So be patient and kind with yourself and find ways to incorporate them into your life that work for you.

My grandmother used to say, "Life is what you make it." I never fully appreciated the deeper meaning of that saying until recently, especially those last two words: *make it.* To craft and create. To choose. No excuses. No one else is responsible for your peace and joy, and quite frankly, no one else can give them to you. What we make of life, or how we make the best of it, is the essence of acceptance.

We all tell ourselves stories about what is or how we wish things were. It's time to change the narrative and manage ourselves better by applying the power of flexibility to our lives.

With that in mind, let's end with a final story.

Moving On

There was a wise man who was visited every day by people seeking advice for their problems. Day after day, they came to his remote hut to complain about all of their troubles, frustrations, and unhappiness. The wise man was patient. He let them complain, then tried to give them advice. However, they still returned to complain again and again. Finally, the wise man decided to try a different approach.

A visitor appeared at his door, a man who had already visited him many times before. He began to complain about his life, the same complaints that he'd shared in the past. So the wise man told him a joke. The man roared with laughter, then resumed complaining.

After a few minutes, the wise man told exactly the same joke again. This time, the man only smiled, then continued complaining.

Finally, the wise man told the same joke for the third time.

This time, the man didn't react at all. No laugh, no smile, nothing.

When the wise man told the joke a fourth time, the man had enough.

"Why do you keep telling the same joke?" he asked. "It was funny the first time, but it's not funny anymore."

"You see that you can't laugh at the same joke over and over," the wise man said, "so why are you always crying about the same problems?"

It's not unlike the two tales we told at the beginning of the chapter. Which wolf are you going to feed? How long are you going to hold the glass? The choice is yours. Embrace acceptance and set the glass down before the weight becomes too much to bear. Stop feeding the angry, resentful wolf and let go of the burden of trying to control what you cannot control.

It's a choice you'll have to make, but know this: Acceptance is the anchor for all of our foundational principles. It makes us sensible, practical, and mature. Acknowledging what *is* and letting go of what *isn't* perpetuates self-control, leniency, and a recognition of reality, which can help us to embody all of the other principles in this book.

The price you pay is worth it, as there is no greater prize in this life than finding sustainable peace and joy.

> *"Things without all remedy*
> *should be without regard:*
> *what's done is done."*
>
> —WILLIAM SHAKESPEARE

Afterword

When I first considered writing this book, I was initially inspired by the shorter and more concise works that I would often keep on my nightstand for reference and, most of all, for comfort. It was in that spirit that I came to believe there might be value in creating a companion or guide that could be both practical and uncomplicated, with universal appeal and timeless insights intended to help readers find a path to lasting peace and joy.

As I shared in the very beginning, this was inspired by my four-year-old niece who, unknown to her, embodied these qualities unselfconsciously on a random Saturday afternoon while playing in the grass beside a soccer field in her colorful unicorn sneakers. The memory of that simple and beautiful afternoon reminds me of one final story I came across during this process. It appropriately captures the essence and magic of the symbol I chose for this book.

To Be Free

A little girl was sitting in art class, creating a drawing in her sketchbook. Her teacher walked by and saw the artwork and asked, "What are you drawing?"

"I'm drawing God," the girl replied.

"But nobody knows what God looks like," the teacher said.

The little girl looked up at her teacher sharply and said, "They will in a minute."

We get inspiration from many sources, but there is something about the lightness of a child in a moment of relaxed and unhampered play that reminds us of what we're striving for: to shrug off the burdens that weigh us down and live freely, joyfully, and at peace.

To achieve that lightness, we must first become solid. We

first need to create a firm foundation on which to build our lives, a foundation that will tell us *who* we are and *how* we can achieve a natural, free-flowing way of life. Of course, we often complicate the process. We're flawed, idiosyncratic, and imperfect, so to achieve lightness, we have to get back to basics and focus on the fundamental qualities that we know to be true. It's been said that perfect people aren't real and real people aren't perfect.

That's where our personal ethics come into play. By combining a set of rare magical traits, we give ourselves focus, remove the gray areas that cause confusion, and condense the qualities of a peaceful, joyful life down to a few principles centered on selflessness.

I believe this is the secret to making ourselves feel solid, whole, and complete, and it's in this place that we brush aside the challenges and worries and achieve a natural state of being.

To be sure, I believe we should take these principles seriously in our lives, but at the same time, we have to be careful not to take *ourselves* too seriously. This is not about purpose or passion but perhaps something less philosophical and abstract. Indeed, the ultimate focus of these five principles is selflessness because an inflated sense of self is at the root of so many of our personal struggles.

Let's remind ourselves of those five foundational principles:

1. Kindness fueled by compassion

2. Gratitude fueled by awareness

3. Integrity fueled by decency

4. Humility fueled by perspective

5. Acceptance fueled by flexibility

It's these five principles that create a solid foundation on which to build the kind of lives that will lead us to a lasting and sustainable peace and joy. Just as importantly, they are principles that we can incorporate into our lives in a way that feels natural and instinctive, without the need for manufactured processes that are difficult to maintain.

These principles have a thread of selflessness that connects them all, as it helps us to understand our place in the world and our purpose for being. It gives us a perspective for viewing the world around us with an attitude of abundance and objectivity.

Our image of the unicorn is a fitting metaphor because these principles connect harmoniously to the associated themes of healing, magic, and grace. They are uplifting, positive principles that make us feel whole by simplifying what matters and allowing us to *let go* of the burdens of self in order to be free.

Focus on the Journey Ahead

Moving forward, it's important to offer some more concrete ways to begin building these principles into your life, so let's finish our journey here together by discussing some simple, practical ideas for incorporating kindness, gratitude, integrity, humility, and acceptance into your daily existence.

Remember, we're not looking back, regretting the past, or dwelling on what could or should have been. Keep your focus on the journey ahead, and you stand a much better chance of releasing old behavior patterns that drag you down. Through deliberate intention, you can become more mindful about integrating these principles into your life. Here are some recommendations for simple, practical ways to begin doing that.

Kindness

Commit to one *intentional* act of kindness for someone every day. It can be a family member, a friend, a coworker, a casual acquaintance, or a complete stranger. It's that simple. Make it a habit and it will start to become a default to your being.

Gratitude

Begin practicing awareness by writing down what you're grateful for each day. You can do this first thing in the morning, during the day, or at night before you go to bed. It's up to you how you do it; just make sure it fits into your life easily.

Integrity

Dedicate yourself to keeping your word about everything you agree to for one week. Do exactly what you say you will do. Although one week might sound easy, try and give proper attention to what this entails and it will help you begin to build your "integrity muscle."

Humility

Make a list of your shortcomings and ways you can improve them. This simple exercise can be very grounding, so remember that being *very* honest with yourself is the way to understanding your *relative* significance and place in the world.

Acceptance

Forgive someone. Chances are, there's someone in your life that you still hold some resentment toward. Today, if you can, decide to be at peace with that person and the circumstances connected to the conflict. This is a positive way of learning to live with reality. By the way, the person you need to forgive might be *yourself*.

Find Your Starting Place

These activities aren't mandatory by any means. If you can think of ways to begin implementing these principles that are more compatible with your life, go for it. This is not intended to be entirely prescriptive but rather more assistive, which is why the ideas shared will give you a starting place if you need one.

Remember to focus particularly on those principles that you find the most challenging. For example, you may struggle to let go of judgment, or you might have a real problem with accepting things as they happen. Perhaps kindness comes easy, but you don't always feel grateful. Maybe you're not as humble as you'd like to be. Whatever the case, find practical ways to address the areas that represent your greatest struggles and begin to include these principles in your everyday life.

I also recommend writing down where you stand with

each of the five virtues currently. This kind of personal inventory or self-assessment can be helpful as you consider the way forward, and it will be encouraging later on as you look back at your growth.

After you do that, consider some examples of how you've seen other people embody these principles heroically. Have you seen an inspiring act of kindness? Have you witnessed a powerful moment of acceptance or a profound expression of gratitude? Do you know someone who lives with and demonstrates the utmost integrity or humility? It can be helpful to write down these precedents so you can meditate and reflect on them. Let them become inspirations that you find motivation to draw from.

It's no secret that our state of being can and will fluctuate. We deal with conflicting emotions and changing circumstances. However, if you can embrace these principles in practical ways, you will begin to resolve the internal conflicts and be able to focus on your personal evolution toward peace and joy.

Ultimately, peace and joy are simply by-products of becoming better humans, which is why the principles we've discussed are focused on how we treat people: both ourselves and others. Life is too short to live with harmful emotions and burdens, so spend your finite time capturing the timeless qualities of kindness, gratitude, integrity, humility, and acceptance.

Is it really that simple?

Of course not. Life is the greatest gift, yet so complicated, and we're all only and simply human. Because of this, we tend to overcomplicate things, so getting back to a few key fundamentals helps us to simplify our thinking and focus our efforts on a direction that is both practical and constructive. It reduces the depths of our issues by distilling them down into a few essential principles that bring us closer to peace and joy.

Regardless of your principles, by coming to know who you are, what you stand for, and what's important to you, you create the possibility for calm, clarity, and contentment, and these, in turn, lay a foundation for peace and joy. Why peace and joy? Because in combination, they give us the harmony and balance we need and enable us to delight in what we have.

Last, understand that peace and joy aren't destinations that bring you to a standstill. On the contrary, we find them along the path so they can become the centerpiece of our next steps in life. Of course, the path doesn't end, so keep moving forward. In time, embracing these foundational principles for your life will lead you to discover the unicorn in you.

Acknowledgments

This endeavor is in many ways the result of all the love I have been fortunate to receive throughout my life. Even though it would be fitting to thank each and every person who has helped to shape me along the way, to do so would in fact last longer than this entire book.

For the purposes here, the following people were especially instrumental over the past year and a half as I managed to gain the confidence to move forward with this project. I am beyond grateful for you all.

To Frances Jane O'Steen and Jeffrey Miller, thank you for your compassionate guidance and patient support in helping me understand what I wanted to say and how to best say it.

All of the kids in my life who make me feel like I am their age and perhaps think that I am: Nicole, Khalil, Alexandra, Chloe, Khadijah, Samantha, Jade, Benjamin, Avery, Kayden, Jacob, Mia, Daniella, Ava, and my unicorn with those colorful sneakers, Keira.

I am thankful for the inspiration and encouragement I received from several women who did so unknowingly but nonetheless did so most meaningfully: Allison Long Pettine, Jennifer Edwards, Judith Sung, Kidada Kendall, Marita Etcubañez, Rachel Sontag, Sapna Werner, and Tamika Smith.

There are a number of close confidants whom I greatly appreciate for offering me such genuine care and heartfelt friendship: Adam Newsome, Andrew Wolf, David Chubinsky, Harold Bollaci, Jordan Roth, Matthew Chubinsky, Seth Bergman, and Todd Finard.

Day in and day out, Jenni Perry, Jennifer Wright, Kathie Wright, and Lisa Carrick make everything possible in my world, and I am keenly aware of how blessed I am to have them as trusted partners and friends.

My family in Miami means more to me than they probably know or believe, and I'm forever grateful for everything that they have done for me, especially Beatrice Winder, Jane Cayemitte, and Marie-Alice Armand.

And to my loving parents, Arthur and Nancy, my devoted sister, Allison, and my special uncle Ed—and very long list of extended relatives—thank you for just about everything, for all my life.

Finally, Selena Dorsey once told me that for me to find peace and joy, it would need to come from within. I think she likely knew I would find it long before I ever believed I could. It was from that unwavering belief, steadfast loyalty, eternal optimism—not to mention her perpetual smile— that I finally learned to trust in the knowing.

To offer one final postscript, if it were acceptable to give a writing credit to a twelve-pound Havanese, then my furry little friend would be so deserving. As he watched me write with seeming approval and endless enthusiasm, I found within myself an unexpected, yet decidedly genuine, sense of peace and joy because of his love. Thanks, Buddy.